Merry Christmas

To: _____

From: _____

Always Believe in the Magic of Christmas

Table of Contents

Deck The Halls 2

Angels We Have Heard On High 3

We Three Kings 4

We Wish You A Merry Christmas 5

Silent Night 7

God Rest Ye Merry Gentlemen 8

The Twelve Days Of Christmas 9

O Come All Ye Faithful 11

Hark! The Herald Angel Sing 12

Jingle Bells 13

The First Noel 15

Away in a Manger 16

Good King Wenceslas 17

Joy To The World 19

O Holy Night 20

O Christmas Tree 22

Ding Dong! Merrily On High 23

Deck The Halls

Deck the hall with boughs of holly
Fa-la-la-la-la, la-la-la-la
Tis the season to be jolly
Fa-la-la-la-la, la-la-la-la
Don we now our gay apparel
Fa-la-la, la-la-la, la-la-la
Troll the ancient Yuletide carol
Fa-la-la-la-la, la-la-la-la

See the blazing Yule before us
Fa-la-la-la-la, la-la-la-la
Strike the harp and join the chorus
Fa-la-la-la-la, la-la-la-la
Follow me in merry measure
Fa-la-la, la-la-la, la-la-la
While I tell of Yuletide treasure
Fa-la-la-la-la, la-la-la-la

Fast away the old year passes
Fa-la-la-la-la, la-la-la-la
Hail the new, ye lads and lasses
Fa-la-la-la-la, la-la-la-la
Sing we joyous all together
Fa-la-la, la-la-la, la-la-la
Heedless of the wind and weather
Fa-la-la-la-la, la-la-la-la

Angels We Have Heard On High

Angels we have heard on high,
Sweetly singing o'er the plains;
And the mountains in reply
Echoing their joyous strains:
Gloria in excelsis Deo,
Gloria in excelsis Deo.

Shepherds, why this jubilee?
Why your joyous strains prolong?
What the gladsome tidings be
Which inspire your heav'nly song?
Gloria in excelsis Deo,
Gloria in excelsis Deo.

Come to Bethlehem and see
Him whose birth the angels sing;
Come adore on bended knee
Christ, the Lord, our newborn King.
Gloria in excelsis Deo,
Gloria in excelsis Deo.

See Him in a manger laid,
Whom the choirs of angels praise;
Mary, Joseph, lend your aid,
While our hearts in love we raise.
Gloria in excelsis Deo,
Gloria in excelsis Deo.

We Three Kings

We three kings of Orient are, Bearing gifts we traverse afar,
Field and fountain, moor and mountain, Following yonder Star.

Chorus:
O, star of wonder, star of might,
Star with royal beauty bright,
Westward leading, still proceeding,
Guide us to the perfect light.

Born a babe on Bethlehem's plain; Gold I bring to crown Him again;
King forever, ceasing never, Over us all to reign.

Chorus

Frankincense to offer have I; Incense owns a Deity nigh;
Prayer and praising, all men raising, Worship Him, God most High.

Chorus

Myrrh is mine; its bitter perfume, Breathes a life of gathering gloom;
Sorrowing, sighing, bleeding, dying, Sealed in the stone-cold tomb.

Chorus

Glorious now behold Him arise, King and God and sacrifice,
Heaven sings, "Hallelujah!" Hallelujah!" The Earth replies.

We Wish You a Merry Christmas

We wish you a merry Christmas
We wish you a merry Christmas
We wish you a merry Christmas and a happy new year
Good tidings we bring to you and your kin
We wish you a merry Christmas and a happy new year

Oh, bring us some figgy pudding [3]
And a cup of good cheer

Good tidings we bring to you and your kin
We wish you a merry Christmas and a happy new year

We won't go until we get some [3]
So bring it right here

Good tidings we bring to you and your kin
We wish you a merry Christmas and a happy new year

So bring us some figgy pudding [3]
With all its good cheers

Good tidings we bring to you and your kin
We wish you a merry Christmas and a happy new year
We wish you a merry Christmas
We wish you a merry Christmas
We wish you a merry Christmas and a happy new year

Silent Night

Silent night, holy night!
All is calm, all is bright.
Round yon Virgin, Mother and Child.
Holy infant so tender and mild,
Sleep in heavenly peace,
Sleep in heavenly peace.

Silent night, holy night!
Shepherds quake at the sight.
Glories stream from heaven afar
Heavenly hosts sing Alleluia,
Christ the Savior is born!
Christ the Savior is born.

Silent night, holy night!
Son of God love's pure light.
Radiant beams from Thy holy face
With dawn of redeeming grace,
Jesus Lord, at Thy birth.
Jesus Lord, at Thy birth

God Rest Ye Merry Gentlemen

God rest ye merry, gentlemen
Let nothing you dismay
Remember Christ our Savior, Was born on Christmas Day;
To save us all from Satan's power, When we were gone astray

Chorus:
O tidings of comfort and joy, Comfort and joy
O tidings of comfort and joy!

In Bethlehem, in Israel, This blessed Babe was born,
And laid within a manger, Upon this blessed morn;
The which His mother Mary, Did nothing take in scorn.

(Chorus)

From God our heavenly Father, A blessed angel came;
And unto certain shepherds, Brought tidings of the same;
How that in Bethlehem was born, The Son of God by name.

(Chorus)

"Fear not, then," said the angel, "Let nothing you afright
This day is born a Savior, Of a pure Virgin bright,
To free all those who trust in Him, From Satan's power and might."

(Chorus)

The shepherds at those tidings, Rejoiced much in mind,
And left their flocks a-feeding, In tempest, storm and wind,
And went to Bethlehem straightaway, The son of God to find.

The 12 Days Of Christmas

On the **FIRST** day of Christmas my true love sent to me
A partridge in a pear tree

On the **SECOND** day of Christmas my true love sent to me,
Two turtle doves and A partridge in a pear tree

On the **THIRD** day of Christmas my true love sent to me,
Three french hens, Two turtle doves and A partridge in a pear tree

On the **FOURTH** day of Christmas my true love sent to me
Four calling birds, Three french hens, Two turtle doves and
A partridge in a pear tree

On the **FIFTH** day of Christmas my true love sent to me,
Five golden rings, Four calling birds, Three french hens,
Two turtle doves and A partridge in a pear tree

On the **SIXTH** day of Christmas my true love sent to me
Six geese a-laying, Five golden rings, Four calling birds,
Three french hens Two turtle doves and A partridge in a pear tree

On the **SEVENTH** day of Christmas my true love sent to me
Seven swans a-swimming, Six geese a-laying, Five golden rings,
Four calling birds Three french hens, Two turtle doves and
A partridge in a pear tree

On the **EIGHTH** day of Christmas my true love sent to me
Eight maids a-milking, Seven swans a-swimming, Six geese a-laying
Five golden rings, Four calling birds, Three french hens
Two turtle doves and A partridge in a pear tree

On the **NINTH** day of Christmas my true love sent to me
Nine ladies dancing, Eight maids a-milking,
Seven swans a-swimming, Six geese a-laying, Five golden rings,
Four calling birds, Three french hens, Two turtle doves and
A partridge in a pear tree

On the **TENTH** day of Christmas my true love sent to me
Ten lords a-leaping, Nine ladies dancing, Eight maids a-milking
Seven swans a-swimming, Six geese a-laying
Five golden rings, Four calling birds, Three french hens
Two turtle doves and A partridge in a pear tree

On the **ELEVENTH** day of Christmas my true love sent to me
Eleven pipers piping, Ten lords a-leaping, Nine ladies dancing,
Eight maids a-milking, Seven swans a-swimming,
Six geese a-laying, Five golden rings
Four calling birds, Three french hens
Two turtle doves and A partridge in a pear tree

On the **TWELFTH** day of Christmas my true love sent to me
Twelve drummers drumming, Eleven pipers piping, Ten lords a-leaping
Nine ladies dancing, Eight maids a-milking, Seven swans a-swimming,
Six geese a-laying Five golden rings, Four calling birds
Three french hens, Two turtle doves and
A partridge in a pear tree

O Come All Ye Faithful

O come all ye faithful, joyful and triumphant
Oh come ye, O come ye to Bethlehem
Come and behold Him, born the King of Angels
O come let us adore Him, O come let us adore Him
O come let us adore Him, Christ the Lord

Sing choirs of angels, sing in exultation
Sing all ye citizens of Heaven above
Glory to God, all glory in the highest
O come let us adore Him, O come let us adore Him
O come let us adore Him, Christ the Lord

Yeah, Lord we greet Thee, born this happy morning
Jesus to Thee be all glory given
Word of the Father, now in flesh appearing
O come let us adore Him, O come let us adore Him
O come let us adore Him, Christ the Lord, Christ the Lord

Hark! The Herald Angels Sing

Hark! The herald angels sing
"Glory to the newborn King"
Peace on earth and mercy mild
God and sinners reconcile

Joyful, all ye nations, rise
Join the triumph of the skies
With th' angelic host proclaim
"Christ is born in Bethlehem"

Hark! The herald angels sing
"Glory to the newborn King"

Hail! The Heav'n born Prince of peace!
Hail! The Son of righteousness!
Light and life to all he brings
Risen with healing in His wings

Mild He lays his glory by
Born that Man no more may die
Born to raise the sons of earth
Born to give them second birth

Hark! The herald angels sing
"Glory to the newborn King!"

Jingle Bells

Dashing through the snow
In a one-horse open sleigh
O'er the fields we go
Laughing all the way
Bells on bobtails ring
Making spirits bright
What fun it is to ride and sing
A sleighing song tonight

[Chorus]
Jingle bells, jingle bells
Jingle all the way
Oh, what fun it is to ride
In a one-horse open sleigh, hey
Jingle bells, jingle bells
Jingle all the way
Oh, what fun it is to ride
In a one-horse open sleigh

Now the ground is white
And the night is young
Take the sleigh tonight
And join us in this song
Just get a bobtailed bay
Get ready for a run
Then hitch him to a sleigh
And now we'll have some fun!

The First Noel

The first Noel the angel did say
Was to certain poor shepherds in fields as they lay
In fields where they lay a-keeping their sheep
On a cold winter's night that was so deep
Noel, Noel, Noel, Noel
Born is the King of Israel
They looked up and saw a star
Shining in the east, beyond them far
And to the earth it gave great light
And so it continued both day and night
Noel, Noel, Noel, Noel
Born is the King of Israel
Born is the King of Israel

Away in a Manger

Away in a manger, no crib for a bed
The little Lord Jesus laid down his sweet head
The stars in the bright sky looked down where he lay
The little Lord Jesus asleep on the hay

The cattle are lowing, the baby awakes
But little Lord Jesus, no crying he makes
I love thee, Lord Jesus! look down from the sky
And stay by my cradle till morning is nigh

Be near me, Lord Jesus; I ask thee to stay
Close by me forever, and love me I pray
Bless all the dear children in thy tender care
And take us to heaven to live with thee there

Good King Wenceslas

Good King Wenceslas looked out on the feast of Stephen
When the snow lay round about, Deep and crisp and even,
Brightly shone the moon that night, Though the frost was cruel
When a poor man came in sight, Gath'ring winter fuel

"Hither, page, and stand by me, If thou know'st it, telling
Yonder peasant, who is he?, Where and what his dwelling?"
"Sire, he lives a good league hence, Underneath the mountain
Right against the forest fence, by Saint Agnes' fountain."

"Bring me food and bring me wine, Bring me pine logs hither
Thou and I will see him dine When we bear him thither."
Page and monarch forth they went, Forth they went together
Through the cold wind's wild lament, And the bitter weather

"Sire, the night is darker now, And the wind blows stronger
Fails my heart, I know not how, I can go no longer."
"Mark my footsteps, my good page, Tread thou in them boldly
Thou shalt find the winter's rage, Freeze thy blood less coldly."

In his master's steps he trod, Where the snow lay dinted
Heat was in the very sod, Which the Saint had printed
Therefore, Christian men, be sure, Wealth or rank possessing
Ye who now will bless the poor, Shall yourselves find blessing

Joy To The World

Joy to the world, the Lord is come
Let earth receive her King
Let every heart prepare Him room
And Heaven and nature sing
And Heaven and nature sing
And Heaven and Heaven and nature sing
Joy to the world, the Savior reigns
Let men their songs employ
While fields and floods
Rocks, hills and plains
Repeat the sounding joy
Repeat the sounding joy
Repeat, repeat, the sounding joy
He rules the world with truth and grace
And makes the nations prove
The glories of His righteousness
And wonders of His love
And wonders of His love
And wonders, wonders, of His love

O Holy Night

O Holy night! The stars are brightly shining
It is the night of our dear Savior's birth
Long lay the world in sin and error pining
'Til He appears and the soul felt its worth
A thrill of hope the weary world rejoices
For yonder breaks a new and glorious morn
Fall on your knees; O hear the Angel voices!
O night divine, O night when Christ was born
O night, O Holy night, O night divine!

Led by the light of Faith serenely beaming
With glowing hearts by His cradle we stand
So led by light of a star sweetly gleaming
Here come the Wise Men from Orient land
The King of kings lay thus in lowly manger
In all our trials born to be our friend
He knows our need, to our weakness is no stranger
Behold your King; before Him lowly bend
Behold your King; before Him lowly bend

Truly He taught us to love one another;
His law is love and His Gospel is Peace
Chains shall He break, for the slave is our brother
And in His name, all oppression shall cease
Sweet hymns of joy in grateful chorus raise we
Let all within us Praise His Holy name
Christ is the Lord; O praise His name forever!
His power and glory evermore proclaim
His power and glory evermore proclaim

O Christmas Tree

O Christmas Tree, O Christmas tree,
 How lovely are your branches!
O Christmas Tree, O Christmas tree,
 How lovely are your branches!
 Not only green in summer's heat,
 But also winter's snow and sleet.
O Christmas tree, O Christmas tree,
 How lovely are your branches!
O Christmas Tree, O Christmas tree,
 Of all the trees most lovely;
O Christmas Tree, O Christmas tree,
 Of all the trees most lovely.
 Each year you bring to us delight
 With brightly shining Christmas light!
O Christmas Tree, O Christmas tree,
 Of all the trees most lovely.
O Christmas Tree, O Christmas tree,
 We learn from all your beauty;
O Christmas Tree, O Christmas tree,
 We learn from all your beauty.
Your bright green leaves with festive cheer,
Give hope and strength throughout the year.
O Christmas Tree, O Christmas tree,
 We learn from all your beauty.

Ding-Dong! Merrily On High

Ding dong, merrily on high!
In heav'n the bells are ringing;
ding dong, verily the sky
is riv'n with angel singing.
Gloria, hosannah in excelsis!
Gloria, hosannah in excelsis!

E'en so here below, below,
let steeple bells be swungen,
And io, io, io,
by priest and people sungen.
Gloria, hosannah in excelsis!
Gloria, hosannah in excelsis!

Pray ye dutifully prime
your matin chime, ye ringers;
may ye beautifully rhyme
your evetime song, ye singers.
Gloria, hosannah in excelsis!
Gloria, hosannah in excelsis!

Printed in Dunstable, United Kingdom